ATTRAVERSIAMO

WORDS FROM THE SOUL

PREMKUMAR RAJAGOPAL

Contents

Contents

"ATTRAVERSIAMO"

Language – English

1 St Edition in 2022

Cover & Manuscript by – R. PREM KUMAR

Compiled By – R. PREM KUMAR

Acknowledgements

This book is published under Notion Press being compiled by R. PREM KUMAR.

Thanks to NOTION PRESS PUBLICATIONS for their support in this process.

We are thankful to our "Amazing Co-Authors" for pouring out their wonderful and heart touching poetries under this book.

Disclaimer

"ATTRAVERSIAMO" is my second book under Notion Press and is totally a work of fiction and the amazing imaginations of our amazing writers. All the thoughts, writings were been penned by the imaginative purpose of the writers itself.

We do not take any responsibilities in case of plagiarism of content found as neither of publication, founders or the compilers would be responsible for this. The writers will be the sole source of the above same

1. COMPILER

He is R. Prem Kumar. He cleared National Eligibility Test for Assistant professors (NET) in 2019. Currently, he is a Ph.D. research scholar at The Gandhigram Rural Institute, Dindigul. He has published a book 'Greek Mythology: A Postmodern Retelling' in Notion Press. He has also published 10 research articles in journals and books. He has published a poem

'Enduring Memories' in the anthology Saccharine Juncture'. He is the admin of the literary meme page 'NET/SET/JRF ENGLISH LITERATURE. (Facebook /Instagram) He is a review committee member of three International journals. Other than academic writing he likes to write poems and short stories. Instagram - Premkumar_rajagopal / net-set-jrf-english-literature Facebook - Premkumar Rajagopal / NET/SET/JRF ENGLISH LITERATURE

2. JOURNEY TO UNLOVE

I conveyed my wish to live with you years before.
Accept me; Reject me; Throw away;
Or
Explain me that you're not mine;
Elucidate the causes for your hatred towards me;
Ignore me as my love is just an infatuation;
Cut me with the power of your words;
You own the rights.
But,
Never, try to condemn my love for you
Or
Ask me to unlove you,
Remember...
You don't have any rights for that...
As you know,
Atheists cannot condemn the existence of gods.

3. Aravindasankar S S

*He is Aravind. He is a Graduate of English Literature &
Currently pursuing a Master's in Business Administration, He is
an Enthusiastic, Good Passionate speaker & Bibliophile, who is
also very fond of representing Literature oriented activities in
both English & Tamil Language, and won literary competitions.
His whole strength depends on his words & kindness. He will
accomplish all his missions and overcome the virtues by his own
effort.*

You can ping him via his Instagram Handle: aravind_dhonist

4. Unforgettable Person

Sequence Classrooms; Dark Black Boards
Benches and Chalk piece too
Books and Notes with Pens;
That all reminds me of you
Multiple Pillars stood next to windows
Nature and sky wanders;
That all reminds me of you
Poems in English; Finishing with Great diction
That all reminds me of you;
Skits and Parades enacted by you; seen all or a few
Dialogues recited on stages; Reaches near the judges
That all reminds me of you;
Designer accouters with Sparkling Zuries
Decorated with Flowers in your hair
That all reminds me of you
Silly Jokes daft some one
Not at all fine; having long gone
That all reminds me of you
Tears in Night rage that takes
Flashes in my speeches
That all reminds me of you;
Now you are gone and I'm falling on,

I got sigh, and I pine,
I miss what was mine
The world reminds me of you.
© *Aravindasankar S S*

5. Satyam Pandit

He is a man who loves trying new things and feels life to the fullest. He started writing in 6th grade and it started with an experience when he was unable to explain but wrote it beautifully. He loves reading and writing, He wrote a lot of poems, mostly on motivation and culture, and also short stories containing his day to day experiences and explorations of the world around him.

Instagram Handle:
https://instagram.com/__satyampandat?r=nametag
E-mail: 7atyam.5andit1997@gmail.com

6. SHE

Her crooked lips and compelling brown eyes, takes me closer and
closer to the skies.
The lines on her neck and her soft white skin, makes me feel little
dim.
Her sonorous mellifluous voice, my ear's personal choice.
The dimples on her cheeks and on the left of her nose, that mole,
touch my soul.
The fragrance of her light black hair makes me to dare. Traps my
soul inside it,
And that's not fair.
My devotion and desire is fierce as fire. Deeper as the ocean,
graceful as sapphire.
Yes I do flirt, but you are the only one closer to my HEART..
© Satyam Pandit

7. Shayila Farhandha O B

She is Shayila. She completed M.A. English Literature at Bharathiar University and cleared UGC NET in 2020 and 2021. She is an extrovert, a good speaker, a listener and observer, and easy going person. As a literature student, She loves reading books. Reading books helped her to create literary memes which

became a platform to communicate with like-minded people on social media. She feels writing is a therapy and it works as defense mechanism in her life. And this write-up, Our First meeting is the spark of her feelings that she couldn't resist and poured into words.

Follow her on Instagram @literaturethroughmemes.

8. Our first Meeting

He is her real life fantasy.
The moment when she glanced at him,
A butterfly flutters around her.
She is the most innocent soul with gleaming eyes,
Shyness scattered with a cute smile.
Rather than, finding the perfect so she finds a weird imperfect
guy,
Who is imperfectly perfect for her.
He standing with a cup of milk in his hand and
almost going to sip the last drop of milk
with his honeyed lips.
Then she approached him closer
That moment
she feels like time stood still on the soul of
the world surged within her.
He looked into her mesmerizing eyes,
he notices her lips for poised between a laugh
and silence.
When did two pairs of eyes meet,
she forgets everything even her existence.
She feels like he engulfs her.
And he feels like something is knocking at his ribs

to hold her and never ever leave.

They both fallen for each other unexpectedly.

He realised that he loved her before he knew that she existed.

And she feels that he deserves her.

Like an Island she is surrounded by his love and can't able to

escape.

Love is the pure language,

which doesn't need any explanation

like the universe needs none as it travels through endless time…

© **Shayila Farhandha O B**

9. Sarrveshwaran T P

Born as a natural admirer, Sarrveshwaran takes pleasure in observing the things that go unnoticed. He finds peace in his solitary ramblings on a silent night. He mostly writes striking captions for pictures and shortly feel good poems.

You can read his write-ups from his Instagram page @sarrvi_lyricist.
Yeah, You guessed it right from his handle name. You can find few of the songs that he wrote lyrics for.

10. The presence in absence

I find fragments of you
As I go for my morning walk.
Lingering slowly from behind,
As if I can almost hear you talk.
The glass I broke accidentally on that day,
Scattered into pieces on the floor.
And I hurt myself cleaning the shards,
But I did not see you enter through the door.
On some busy mornings, as I stand
And brush my hair in front of the mirror,
My hand suddenly stops for a second,
As my eyes don't see you over my shoulder.
On some late nights, I hug my pillow
My tears adoring it wet.
And I don't know why but I keep playing
Our memories to the day we met.
Most peoples' sleep are easily prone
To their fears, demons or past.
But your heavenly eyes alone
Haunts me darling, till the night can last.
©Sarrveshwaran T P

11. M. LOGESH BABU

He is Logesh Babu, Ph.D. Research Scholar (English) at BIHER, Chennai who grew to be a Marxist, Ambedkarist, and Periyarist after encountering salient prolonged cruel oppressions laid on the voiceless subalterns of Tamilnadu right from his childhood where his pen thought not to fight but to wage in wrath practicing Red, Blue and Black against Arya Dharma or Sanatana Dharma. Instagram: logesh_babu_m

12. For the Exuberant Pearl

I'm here to pamper you with all my heart, and unconditional love. You are neither my soul nor my soul mate for you're my absolute.

And let us transcend together to manifest our own planet in our tiny little home, with no kids for us.

For I don't want to earn any envy from our babies, making them jealous pampering my beloved the most rather than them.

I lament being an atheist all these days, making discourses on stages ironically.

Charging the existential factor of God and you made me realise that you are my shrine and the absolute in it.

I have never seen you smiling that's your thing but from my side I'm telling you my love, for one drop tear that rolls on your cheek, I'm not a man at all.

I just wanted my Queen to know this, my zealous and ardent love for her. While counting our bodily wrinkles I'll make you realise that no one can love you more than me even your Mother.

©M. LOGESH BABU

13. Radha S

She is Radha S from Chennai, at present, she is working as an Assistant Professor at Sriram College of Arts and Science and also NSS Programme Officer. She is pursuing Ph.D. at Bharat University. Serving others is her passion and part of her life. Perseverance, self-confidence, and hard work are the secrets of her success. She always believes in herself.

ATTRAVERSIAMO

Instagram: Radha_s78

14. Shedding Tears for my Thundering Love

She is the one who gave me the identity and she is the one who made me search for it today.

Your love is the love that no one can give, that's why I can't forget it.

There are so many things to talk about but you are not around to listen.

No matter who you are, the mind wants to own you, You are not responsible for my disappointment, it is because of the high expectations I placed on you.

Among the many changes, only your memories are the only change that never changes. Your feelings embrace me even though I am untouchable.

All the kisses you gave without hesitation now come and go before my eyes with hesitation.

It was behind your division that I realized which of the happy moments my true happiness was.

I miss feeling happiness without you to share it in happy moments. I will spend my time waiting for you by telling a lie that I am coming.

A broken boat washed ashore in the corner of your mind, you are a broken love float.

All words in love are beautiful but some words make love nuclear. There is no great reason for my pains except your division.

My search is calm with your memories without any gap between truth and reality.

Living only in your memories, how can I forget you. Unbearable burdens are nothing before your memories.

Because we are always together in dreams and memories, we are separate in reality.

There are no tears in my eyes and no shape on your lips, because of one word you said, everything was destroyed and its shape changed.

Day by day your quests come and go, all your memories haunt me because I loved you deeply.

You may fade away in reality, but in my dreams you will never fade away my mind, which knows how to hide, still does not know how to forget you.

You could have easily disappeared from me, just told me and left.

There are thousands of pains, there are no words to cry, only tears from my eyes hurt because you left me as my pains.

©Radha S

15. AISWARYA LAKSHMI

To work in a globally competitive environment on challenging task which suits her qualification and domain knowledge that stimulates personal and organizational growth by being efficient and extending the fullest cooperation. She is a self-motivated teacher with over 4 years of teaching experience. Exemplary leadership qualities, the ability to oversee multiple projects and tasks at any given moment, and the ability to work with people from varying backgrounds while implementing team values. Currently, she is working in IISJ, Tokyo, Japan. Pursuing Ph.D. in Bharath Institute of Higher Education and Research, Chennai. Have worked as an Assistant Professor of English and Placement Soft Skill Trainer at New Prince Shri Bhavani Arts and Science College from June 2019 to April-2022.

Instagram: AAiswaryasakthi

16. Memories that Enchants Forever

Cherishing the day you happened into my life
Have been searching for but you strife
Life began the day, love, just we started
Still not changed even you departed
love our crazy memories, make smile, forever
trust our sweet memories, never die, forever
believed, the most treasured heirlooms
Distances not mattered, nostalgia are sweet abloom
You might changed but the memories you gave
Still remember the first day, we connected as beehive
Love for you is eternal, unconditional
It grows stronger and multifunctional
Cherish you with old memories, I adore you
Need you by my side now, I believe you
Recollections are better than the real, I'm reliving
Tears or smiles, dry or fades, I'm falling and outliving
Millions of hallucinations that our love to refine
Hundreds of secrets, love, a reason you're mine
A yearning desire here to hear from you
Loved, lived, the past, leading the present, thank you

Miss our conversations, miss how we together
Every minute of every day, worse we're untogether
My soul as a complete wardrobe lasts forever
My words cannot express the deep love, you're misbeliever
Rain hides the tears, I wish, I could
remove the memories but I determined to live.
*© **AISWARYA LAKSHMI***

17. Naseena Fathima

Naseena Fathima is a PhD research scholar at NSS Training College Ottappalam, Palakkad. She is residing at Kaimalassery, Malappuram District, Kerala. She is an ardent lover of reading and writing.
Instagram: Naseenaputhuparambil

18. I Do Move On

Once, You are my feeling,
You are my thoughts,
You are my inspiration,
Your presence, words, and glances,
Took me to a world of solace.
Now,
Everything is in chaos.
There slowly grows a chasm,
Between you and me...
It took me to a world of darkness
A world of thick darkness.
I can't see anything
But dark clouds loomed over my sky
And set for a heavy rain
I can't hear anything
A word of console
From your lips,
Nothing else brings down
Pangs of pain in my heart...
****

You have gone,
From my love,

ATTRAVERSIAMO

From my despair,
From my delight,
You took my pleasure with you too
Without leaving anything behind,
A little bit of joy or solace…
But I can't live in anguish
I felt nothing but hope and hope,
With that, I will fizzle my sorrows out.
Hope is the guiding star
Which lifts me to the shore of light.
Now,
I slammed the door of my heart
Against you.
I do move on.
Yet,
Haunting memories pinch my heart….
© **Naseena Fathima**

19. A. Balaji

He is a poet wannabe who happens to be a tech-savvy teacher. A proud alum of Gandhigram Rural Institute. A proud Tirunelveli Tamilan. Passionate about literature, music, and photography. GOT, LOTR, and PS-I fanatic

Instagram: @apebalaji

20. Love That Dare Not Speak Its Name

I met him after ten or more years,

He picked me up from the metro in his car,

Our conversation just continued from where we left years ago,

Him mocking my looks, me mooning over his fit and lithe body,

How wrong was I to think "I have forgotten his face and him".

His baritone voice bewitched me just as it did in those days,

I couldn't take off my eyes from magic woven by

His caramel skin, sharp angle eyebrows and Nordic walking.

His cinnamon proximity was aphrodisiac to me,

If he knew it, he didn't show it in his face,

It had been awhile we met; so we talked,

We went to watch a historical fantasy we both read as teenagers,

I arched my brows loudly when he bought tickets and popcorn,

He defended his honour that he did buy snacks at all times,

My heart pitter-pattered every time he helped elderly find their

seat in darkness,

His whispers in my ears, his joyous shouts at on-screen action

undid me, We both knew we shared the same straw for Pepsi

And laughed it off as it was nothing but we both knew it wasn't,

We critiqued the story, gleefully adored the beauty on the screen,

*Then we went to the Burger King and fixed us the biggest
burgers,*
All good things must come to an end; so did ours,
*He just blurted out, "I just couldn't give you the one thing you so
wanted from me",*
*My joyous steps faltered and said "I know and I understand it
now as I aged",*
*After a beat of silence, I said "I hope you didn't resent me for
those days" He instantly stated, "Never" and we stared at each
other to see the truth in our eyes.*
He got a migraine thanks to the ice cream I ordered for him,
*I stuck my tongue at him and he just laughed; I know I had to
let him go,*
*He ordered a cab for me and paid for it, before I leave thrust a
bag at me,*
It was the latest Twilight novel I so waited for.
*In its first page, he signed with "Love you for being my best
friend"*
©A. Balaji

21. G Dhanusree

G Dhanusree is from Chennai. She is a student of Velammal currently pursuing her 7th grade. She has an interest in poetry writing and regularly participates in inter-school competitions. Her other hobbies include portrait drawing.

22. Sweet Memories

My first step in the flight
It made my face bright
I saw the cracker's might
When I burst them in night.
The Blossom of my flower
Bath I took in the river
Thrill at the top of the tower
Peaks wrapped with snow cover
Kiss of the water in the beach
Interesting ways my teacher teach
Delivery of my first speech
Excitement in the goals I reach
These are moments I cherish
Life moves in a flourish
It aids my health nourish
Makes my existence lavish

• ©G Dhanusree

23. V. ABISHEKH

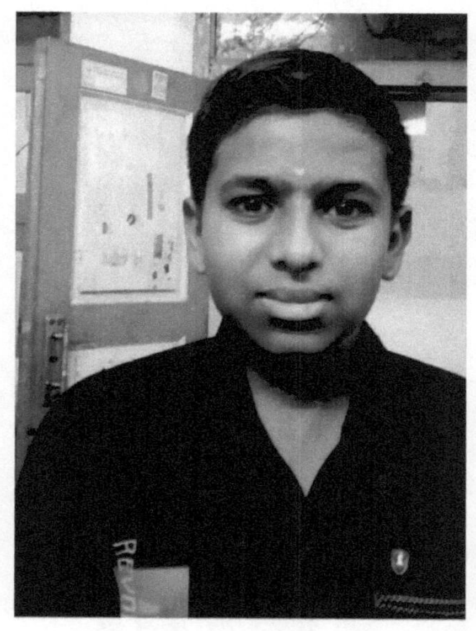

He is a grade 9 student at SBK Boys Higher Secondary School, Aruppukottai. He has an interest in Writing poetry, Cycling, and Skating.

24. MOTHER'S LOVE

You care for me,
Even in your illness.
You play with me,
Putting all your work aside.
You make me smile,
Hiding your problems.
You feed me more,
Even in your hunger.
You are the GOD to me.
Yes…
People call you MOTHER.
© V. Abishekh

25. V. NIVETHITHA

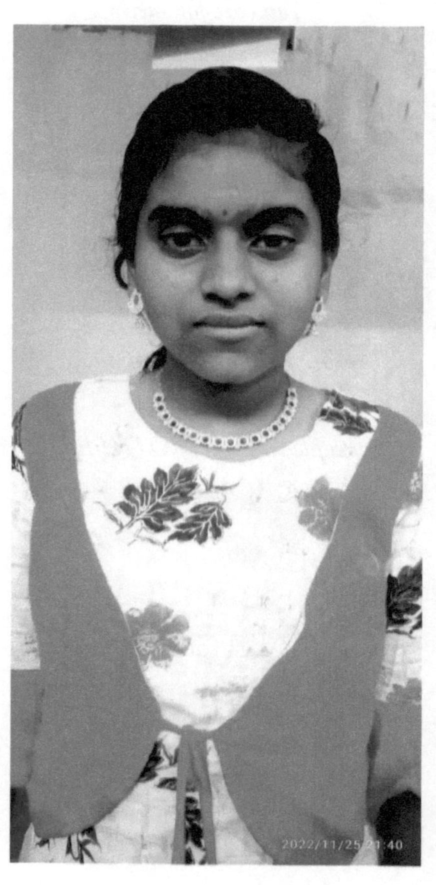

V. Nivethitha is from Aruppukottai. She is a student of SBK Girls Higher Secondary School pursuing 8th grade. She has interest in poetry writing and regularly participates in inter-school competitions. Her other hobbies include portrait drawing.

26. My Mother

My Mother

You are the symbol of love,
Where you smile for my happiness.
I feel the love and tenderness,
In the warmth of your hug.
You will listen to my blabbering,
Like Upanishads.
You work hard for me,
Over your needs.
Even Oceans and Mountains,
Cannot compete your sacrifices.
© V. Nivethitha

www.ingramcontent.com/pod-product-compliance
Lightning Source LLC
Chambersburg PA
CBHW031515150726
47990CB00007B/3027